Broadstair
Heydays and No

Main Bay, Broadstairs c1895.

Bygone Publishing

First published in 2007 by Bygone Publishing, Whitstable, Kent CT5 1WT

A catalogue record for this book is available from the British Library

ISBN 978-0-9545252-6-2

Printed and bound in Great Britain by Geerings Print Ltd, Ashford, Kent

Front cover shows Viking Bay (main bay), on a packed summer day in 1954.

Contents

Introduction

"I don't think we can do better than Good Old Broadstairs!" exclaims Charles Pooter in The Diary Of A Nobody when asked where he wishes to spend his summer holidays. It was a wise choice as countless generations will readily agree. Among them were Princess, later Queen, Victoria and writer Charles Dickens who both put the town on the map.

Despite such worthy patronage Broadstairs was considered rather bourgeois – yet a cut above its neighbours Margate and Ramsgate.

Broadstairs is steeped in history and traces its origins back hundreds of years. A shrine to St Mary of Bradstowe originally brought pilgrims seeking cures to ailments here. The local economy centred around fishing and farming with nearby St Peter's proving the more affluent partner.

Mr Pooter would be astonished at just how much – or indeed how little – Broadstairs and its surrounding villages have changed from their heydays to nowadays. For example, long gone are many of the convalescent homes and private schools with their sprawling estates. Instead, we have housing estates of many shapes and sizes.

Although there are more than 180 illustrations contained herein, they can only be a small selection of the many which have been made over the years. Most of them have been arranged in such a way to enable you to take this book with you on a walk, ride or a drive around the area to see the places for yourself.

Nick Evans
Whitstable
August 2007

Dozens of small craft lie on the sand at low tide beside Broadstairs jetty sometime in the late 1960s. Judging by the emptiness of the beach, the picture was taken on a quiet day. At this time, it was quite easy to hire a boat for a day's angling – in centuries gone by fishermen sailed as far as Iceland for cod.

Broadstairs jetty is thought to be the oldest in England, dating from the reign of King Henry VIII. It was built in 1538 by local benefactor and shipbuilder George Culmer to enable local fishermen to shelter their vessels. The jetty was rebuilt early in the 19th century and we see it here about 100 years after.

There were fewer boats and fewer promenaders on the jetty when this picture was taken in summer 2007 but it is still a focal point for visitors and residents of Broadstairs. People park their cars on it, enjoy ice creams, take lungfuls of bracing sea air from it – and occasionally steal a kiss or two here!

Broadstairs had a succession of lifeboats between 1850 and 1912 when the RNLI closed the base. In that time three vessels were used, saving a total of 269 lives. This is the Christopher Waud Bradford launching on another mission. It saw service between 1888 and 1896 and was replaced by the Francis Forbes Barton.

An Avon Red Cat became the latest addition to the council's fleet of safety boats watching over swimmers at Broadstairs in 1969. Named Stella Maris, it was launched on 4 May by Sir Edward Heath, a year before he became Prime Minister. Here chief boatman Jim Warburton is ready for action in this 1972 view.

The timber boat house stands at the shore end of the jetty and is thought to be at least 300 years old. The harbour master occupies the upper right hand room and has a panoramic view over the sea. From this 1964 view, we can see that half hour sea trips cost four shillings (20p) for adults.

In this 2007 view, the building has a slightly different colour scheme but the red phone box remains in place. Hercules' head and accompanying whale bones have been moved to the left hand side of the building. The Highland Chief (inset) was restored in 2004 and boasts a smart uniform and new shoes.

Bleak House, originally Fort House, was built in 1801 as a private residence and was extended to its present size 100 years later. It's best known as Charles Dickens' holiday home after he stayed there between 1843 and 1851. Once open as a museum in the 1980s, it is now again a private house and suffered a fire in 2006.

Dickens Week in June is the annual celebration of the author's connections with the town and for many years a highlight was a costumed gathering in the gardens of Bleak House. This 1964 view shows the event in full swing. The earliest part of the building can be seen on the right.

Broadstairs Pavilion is the town's premier entertainment venue and was built in 1933, a few years after the council bought the Garden on the Sands upon which it stands. Pictured here in 1960, the pavilion was the summer home of Cecil Barker and his orchestra for many years who played twice daily.

Now part of the Thorley Taverns chain, the pavilion's verandah is a popular place for a quiet drink on a sunny day. The pavilion becomes an important base for shows during the town's Folk Week in August and monthly craft fairs have proved popular for a number of years.

The York Gate was built originally in 1540 by George Culmer soon after work on the jetty was completed. The archway supported a portcullis and heavy gates to prevent pirates attacking the town. Further up on the left is the Palace Cinema, formerly the Windsor, which was built from a boathouse in 1911.

Lord Henniker restored the gateway in 1795 as insurance against a French incursion and his name is borne in an inscription on one side of the stone work. The traditional café and milk bar, owned by the Anselmi family for more than 50 years, gave way to a pizzeria back in 2002.

Marchesi's Restaurant, which fronts Albion Street, was founded in 1886 by Swiss born Frederico Marchesi as a bakery and patisserie and evolved into one of Thanet's best known restaurants. The restaurant's tea garden was doing brisk business when this 1920s picture was captured.

Descendants of Frederico Marchesi, the Roger family, ran the restaurant for many years and 2005 marked the end of a two year long renovation programme. Rightly, they prided themselves on serving high quality cuisine but decided to sell to new owners by the end of that year. Inset is the front of the building.

The Royal Albion Hotel started as the Phoenix but was renamed in1805 in honour of Nelson's victory at Trafalgar. This view is thought to date from 1930 but was used in 1950s adverts. In 1958 bed and breakfast was 25 shillings (£1.25). Next door, the Omar Café was renowned for its bespoke Omar Khayyam wallpaper.

Trust House Hotels owned the Albion for many years before selling to the Roger family in the early 1980s and they in turn sold to Shepherd Neame in 2006. One end of the hotel was where Dickens wrote part of Nicholas Nickleby in 1839 and he returned here in 1840, 1845, 1849 and 1859.

One of the prime movers in starting the annual Dickens Festival Week in 1937 was Miss Gladys Waterer, seen here at the gate of Dickens House in Victoria Parade, then her home, in 1964. She filled the house with many of her hero's possessions. The house was once the home of Miss Mary Strong upon whom the author based his character Betsy Trotwood when writing David Copperfield. Following Miss Waterer's death, aged 85, in January 1971, Dickens House and its historic contents were bequested to the town's council.

The house was opened to the public as a museum during Dickens Festival Week in June 1973, the official ceremony being performed by Peter Dickens, a great grandson of the novelist. Now the museum also houses the Broadstairs Visitor Information Centre. Parts of the house date from Tudor times.

Thousands of pictures showing Viking Bay at the height of summer contrast this 1958 view of a snow covered beach without a soul in sight. The all wooden beach café in the left foreground was lost in a fire in the mid 1970s.

Another wintery shot taken at the same time along Victoria Parade which overlooks the main bay. A couple of hardy souls have braved the snow but are probably deciding against a walk on the beach itself. In the distance is the Grand Hotel and on the far left Victoria clock tower.

This Edwardian post card shows donkeys about to carry their riders on another walk along the beach while, nearby, a group of youngsters builds a sandcastle. The chair would have had upturned lids from shoe polish tins attached to the base of each leg to stop it from sinking in the sand – an early deck chair perhaps?

Donkey rides have never completely lost their appeal and, in the left hand photo, we see children on their steeds in 1969 when the donkeys were operated by Ron Saunders. Today, Alex, Sandy and their handler wait for their lift home at the end of a busy day at the start of the 2007 season.

For many years Peter Buchard was the traditional Punch & Judy man at Viking and Joss Bays. Performances were given twice daily throughout the season and were preceded by a walk around the beach gathering up his young audience Pied Piper style. In 1967, his was definitely the way to do it.

It's enough to bring a tear to the eye! These girls would have been the dancers in the summer show at the town's Bohemia Theatre in 1954. Although they are slightly out of focus, the rarity of six girls doing the splits together on the busy sands at Viking Bay makes it special.

Wearing winged helmets and authentic dress, a contingent of 50 Vikings sailed from Esjberg in Denmark aboard the replica sailing ship Hugin to land at Broadstairs main bay on 28 July 1949. On their rough ten day crossing the men, who all grew beards specially, lived on board as their ancestors did. They were marking the 1,500th anniversary of the Danish invasion of Britain, the traditional landing of Hengist and Horsa and the betrothal of Hengist's daughter Rowena to King Vortigern of Kent.

Around 30,000 people crowded the beach, renamed Viking Bay in honour of the occasion, to see the Hugin land. Formal and informal celebrations with the Danes followed. Police controlling crowds used radios for the first time. In 1950 the ship was set up on the cliffs at Pegwell Bay and was extensively restored in 2005.

Taken from the main steps down to the beach in the early 20th century, we can only guess at what the large crowd is enjoying. It's most likely to be Punch & Judy but could easily be a Sunday prayer service on the sands which was a common sight during summers of 100 years ago.

The concrete verandah and two levels of beach huts were built at the foot of the cliff in the 1930s and proved an immediate success. In this 1954 scene the clock tower stands sentinel. It was given to the town in the early 20th century by local MP Harry H Marks and was rebuilt in1977 after a fire by Thanet College students.

Mario Morelli opened his first ice cream parlour and cappuccino bar on the seafront at Broadstairs in 1932 and here are some of the staff working with him at the time. Both ice cream and cappuccino, then a rarity, were made on site and the business quickly became a success.

Guiseppe Morelli took over from his father in the 1950s and redeveloped the parlour in 1959, making it the first of its kind in Britain, and offering 20 flavours of ice cream. Its original styling has changed little in nearly half a century but management passed to Mario's grandson Marino in 1972.

VelvaCream ice cream was synonymous with Morellis and this Austin van, with Giuseppe and dog posing alongside, was a familiar sight around Thanet during the 1950s. Now a fleet of Morelli refrigerated vehicles delivers 200,000 items of food from a factory in Minster to 25 franchised outlets around the UK each week.

The black-knobbed circular ashtrays on the tables inside Morellis are the only real giveaways to the true age of this photo. This 1959 view is little different to the modern scene as the ornate ceiling, the mirrored serving area and the Lloyd Loom chairs are still much in evidence. It's not retro, it's original.

Bracing sea air was a certainty as you walked along the promenade in Edwardian times. The Victoria Gardens were opened by Princess Louise in 1832 and have remained popular ever since. Later on, the town council purchased the gardens which then became Broadstairs' first official park.

Moving further along the road, we can see an elderly lady being towed in her bath chair by a young man in this early 20th century view. The crowd seems intent on gathering around the band stand for a concert while across the bay, barges, possibly colliers, rest on the sand while the tide is out.

The ornate 1887 Victoria Jubilee bandstand was a focal point for many visitors wanting to relax lazily and watch the world go by in this early 1920s view. Note the young lady on the right, dressed in white, who, with ticket machine and collecting bag, takes the money for deck chair hire.

At one time the bandstand was moved and raised to a site nearer Victoria Parade but was relocated to its present site in 1952, about 50 metres from where it was originally, while the surrounding area was relandscaped (see inset). The building on the left is now a residential home and the other forms apartments.

No history of Broadstairs would be complete without mention of Uncle Mack and his troupe of minstrels who entertained for many years. Uncle Mack is on the extreme left in this 1935 photo with, from left, comedian Uncle Jock, tenor Uncle John, pianist Uncle Harry, comedian Uncle Tom and baritone Uncle Alf.

Uncle Mack, JH Summerson, brought joy and laughter to Broadstairs between 1895 and 1948. He died in 1949. Public subscriptions paid for this memorial stone, located in Victoria Gardens, in 1950 when council Chairman Fred Salt and actress Annette Mills, of Muffin The Mule fame, jointly unveiled it before a big crowd.

Broadstairs Folk Week has been held every August since 1965 and is now one of the largest of its kind in Britain. Here, the Hartley Men's Morris entertain in Pierremont Gardens c1991. Since then, as it has grown, the event has switched to the larger Victoria Gardens for some of the headline attractions.

Clarence the dragon has been scaring small children since Folk Week began – in his younger days he breathed smoke too but has given up the habit. Offering up his next snack in 1991 is children's team manager Sonia Stockwell, a stalwart who ran the Hobbyhorse Club for many years until she died in 2006.

A putting green has existed on the corner of Granville Road with Victoria Parade for at least 80 years. Known these days as Lilly-putt, it was run by Pat Regan in the 1950s when 18 holes cost just 6d. A decade before, Jack Nunn charged 4d (2p). Competitions, with prizes, between guest houses were a regular attraction.

An Isle of Thanet Electric Company tram picks up a passenger on Victoria Parade before clattering around the corner to Granville Road. Trams ran between Westbrook, near Margate, and Ramsgate between 1901 and 1937 until East Kent's buses took over. The main tram depot was at St Peter's.

An Edwardian stylised view of the Grand Hotel set atop the cliffs of Louisa Bay. The town's premier hotel, it was built in 1882 for £78,000. The Grand boasted 110 bedrooms plus reading rooms, smoking rooms and billiard hall. In 1938 the hotel held four AA stars and a week's stay cost nine guineas (£9.45) per person.

Later on, the hotel gave way to become the Grand Mansions apartments while the ballroom became the town's leading entertainment venue, hosting many functions including civic dinners, dances and Sir Edward Heath's carol concerts. It was demolished in the 1990s to make way for a trendy block of flats.

Louisa Gap is just a short walk from the main bay. Taken in the early 20th century, we can see how close the Grand Hotel was to the beach but stairs were not built down from the bridge until 1905. Originally known as Goodson Stairs, after a local farmer, the gap was renamed after singer Louisa Crampton, daughter of engineer Thomas who built the bridge in 1850.

A more modern view of Louisa Gap captured during the 1960s just after the promenade and cliff defences had been completed. A decade before, the gap was popular with sand sculptors. People showed their appreciation by throwing coins down to them from the cliff top! Luckily, no one was injured.

The Castlemere Hotel on the Western Esplanade was once run by Mrs Margaret Knight-Bruce and Miss Elizabeth Bennett. Composer Sir Richard Rodney Bennett was born here in 1936 – his mother choosing to be with her in-laws at the time. Little Castlemere was the overflow part of the hotel in 1949.

Little Castlemere is now a much extended private house but the main building continued trading until the 1990s. It was extensively rebuilt to become a block of up market apartments in 2003 – happily retaining its distinctive octagonal tower – and still offering lungfuls of healthy sea air.

Dumpton Gap was once known as Dodemayton and was used by local farmers to get to the beach to collect seaweed which they then used as fertiliser on their fields. In 1914 a submarine telephone cable was laid from here, across the Channel, to Ostend. The junction hut is at the top of the slipway.

The modern view shows little change other than the shelter has been removed. The grassy headland is a haven for walkers who would have had quite a surprise in 1968 when an army helicopter landed here for a time. It was on loan to local police, to test its suitability at landing in restricted spaces.

Behind the line of trees lies King George VI Memorial Park – which was part of Ramsgate when this view was taken, looking along South Cliff Parade, in the 1950s. Amid accusations of snobbery, Broadstairs would not agree to take down the low wall fronting the trees and thus kept the two towns divided for walkers.

The wall eventually did come down in the early 1970s when more houses were built along Seven Stones Drive, turning the corner in this contemporary view. The imposing Colbourn Light was completed in 2000 and is supposed to complement North Foreland lighthouse at the other end of Broadstairs.

A tranquil moment as long skirted ladies process down the High Street, perhaps on their way to the beach, in this view from c1905 before the intervention of the car. The road turning away to the left is Charlotte Street. In the foreground, a tearoom is accessed by walking through the confectioner's.

What was once a greengrocer's is now a butcher's on the facing left hand corner. Considerable rebuilding has taken place along this stretch where it meets Serene Place and cars are now quick to take the few spaces here. Opposite, it is now a curry rather than a cuppa that can be enjoyed in the Tamarind restaurant.

Value, civility and satisfaction were the watchwords of draper William Evans, grandfather of the author at 3 Charlotte Street, who traded in Broadstairs for 25 years. Household linens, blankets, towels, summer dresses and beach wear were sold in abundance when this view was taken in 1955.

Evans' draper was sold on to Jack and Margery Park after William's death in 1956 and they ran the business for another 20 years. The shop was then taken over by Blackburn's to sell soft furnishings before becoming Vassoulla Michael's fashionable boutique.

Arguably the most picturesque part of the centre of Broadstairs is Serene Place, just off the High Street at the bottom of the hill. In 1967 there were two shops. Once the Lancaster House tea room, Joyce sold hats while neighbouring Victoriana sold antiques and china. Castle House at the far end was the home of old tyme music hall star Ted Gatty. He was the man who gave Danny La Rue his name. Note the council poster at the bottom right of the photo warning owners they would be fined £5 if their dogs fouled the footways.

These days there is no trace of the two shops having existed. The bay windowed frontages have been removed from 16th century Serene House but it is recognised as an historic building of Kent, bearing a diamond shaped plaque above the front door. The setting is as attractive as ever.

A prestigious drop-head Alvis is the only vehicle in this 1932 scene looking down the High Street. John T May, whose office is on the left, was a local builder and it was with this firm that the father of Prime Minister Sir Edward Heath worked as a carpenter before starting his own business at Kingsgate.

There has been considerable rebuilding of what is now the Nationwide Building Society on the right as both it and the adjoining property have each lost a storey. Still on this side, an old cinema, remembered for its sliding roof, was demolished in the 1950s. The builder's office is a charity shop.

The Bohemia Theatre traces its origins from 1905 when a concert party called the Broadstairs Bohemians performed here. Then the site was known as The Lawn but such was their success, it was renamed The Bohemia and the theatre was built in 1922. The Bohemia burnt down in November 1963 after becoming derelict but was in good order when this view was taken in June 1960. Note the name of Jack Warner, of Dixon of Dock Green fame, on the concert billboards. He had a home at Kingsgate for many years.

Estate agent Terence Painter built his plush offices on the Bohemia site in the 1990s, the last time a complete new building was erected in the High Street. The adjoining building was a gas showroom for many years and is now home to another estate agent.

Slightly further up the hill that is the High Street, this view dates from 1905. On the extreme left is the Providence Strict Baptist Chapel, marked by an ornamental lamp. The flint buildings towards the bottom of the hill were demolished in the 1950s to widen the road. The tram lines turn into Queens Road to Ramsgate.

A row of shops still operates on the right hand side and includes an off licence, a fish & chip shop, an undertaker's and a bank but the Baptist chapel opposite gave way to a bathroom showroom years ago. Gone also are the tram lines and overhead cables. There are a lot of cars parked too!

HILLMAN

AND

HUMBER

DEALERS

ALL MAKES OF CARS SUPPLIED

BROADSTAIRS MOTOR COMPANY LIMITED

HIGH STREET and VERE ROAD, BROADSTAIRS

Cars from a vanished British motor industry were in vogue when this advert appeared in 1956. Arter Brothers ran the garage during the 1930s when German spy Dr Arthur Tester, living at North Foreland, had his black Rolls Royce serviced here along with his Spanish made Hispano Suiza and US built Auburn.

The garage has had a succession of owners over the years and the current one is Pierremonts which has been operating from the site on the corner with Vere Road since 1990. Although petrol is no longer sold, car hire, servicing and MOT testing are all carried out here.

At the bottom of Vere Road, backing on to local houses and a coach & car park are the town's allotments. Having the chance to grow your own food has been important for people for many years and in 1960, the allotments looked well tended. The houses in the background are along Bradstow Way and Crow Hill.

A plethora of bean poles were in place around the allotments in this 2007 view which also emphasises just how much residential development there has been. With a recent resurgence in the popularity of allotments, it is to be hoped this green area will last for many more years.

Standing outside one of the entrances to Pierremont Hall is the town's war memorial. This was dedicated on 16 June 1923 by archdeacon Ven LJ White-Thompson. It had taken £1,000 and five years of vigorous discussion on where to site the Portland Stone memorial before it was finally unveiled.

The council was only able to place the memorial when it bought the lease on Pierremont Hall for £5,500 in 1922. Angry at the slow progress made, a syndicate of four notable citizens bought the building and grounds from owner Dan Mason, the HP Sauce magnate, to resell to the council when it could afford the price.

A Dickens Festival Week has been held in Broadstairs since 1937 and the 70th anniversary was marked in style during 2007. Here, Dickensians gather in their crinolines and frock coats on the steps of Pierremont Hall in 1978 before parading to the Victoria Gardens. A leading light is Lee Ault, pictured extreme right.

Pierremont Hall was built in 1785 as holiday home for Thomas Forsyth and later enlarged by Edward Fletcher. For many summers in the 19th century, the young Princess, later Queen, Victoria stayed here. It became a school and then the offices of the former Broadstairs & St Peter's Urban District Council.

Set opposite the main driveway up to the railway station was the Railway Tavern, a handy place for weary travellers to rest after getting off the train. The London, Chatham and Dover Railway reached Broadstairs in 1862 bringing people to the town in less than two hours from London for the first time.

The pub has since been renamed Cramptons after Thomas Crampton the engineer who was born in Broadstairs. It is part of the Thorley Taverns chain which, coincidentally, has its headquarters just a 10 minute walk away at the former police station in Gladstone Road.

A young boy wearing a school cap turns to eye the camera as this 1930s picture is captured. He and his father are walking up the slope towards the Ramsgate bound, or down side, of the railway station. Before taxis, locals ran a service carrying holidaymakers' luggage on barrows to their digs.

The ornamental belfry was retained in a 1926 rebuild giving the building a distinguished look now. Passengers for the London track used to be able to pay their fares on the other platform but the ticket office was closed there in the late 1960s. Evidently, small boys still find the station has some appeal.

Steps from the pavement on the left gave access to the station from both sides of the bridge, which was rebuilt in May 1901 to give more headroom for tram passengers. Opening this route was delayed for two months for that reason but a warning to stay seated while on the top deck was still necessary.

A Stagecoach East Kent double decker sweeps under the railway bridge with ease on its way to Canterbury. The warning to stay seated has been replaced by a height indicator which the bus will clear by several inches.

Perhaps because of the bridge, shopkeepers on the nearby Broadway regarded themselves as slightly separate from the rest of the High Street and were happy to band into their own traders' association. The town's main Post Office is at the far end of the row on the junction with Grosvenor Road.

Contrasting with the 1930s view opposite, cars wait impatiently at the traffic lights. Behind the Post Office building, now a sorting office, is Crampton Tower, built in 1859 by Thomas Crampton as a key part of the town's first mains water supply system. Out of view on the left is the town's 1970s built library.

The Broadstairs & St Peter's Mail was the town's local paper from 1903 until 1979 and owned by Ramsgate's East Kent Times. The Mail was named in tribute to Lord Northcliffe, founder of the Daily Mail who lived at Reading Street. The town's paper moved to 13 The Broadway in 1910 when its editor was Amos Hickmore.

The Broadway office enabled people to meet the local news reporter, who in the early 1970s included the author's father Bill Evans. The office was sold in 1982, a year after the EKT was taken over by its rival Isle of Thanet Gazette. Since the early 1980s, Neville Tobin has run his barber's business from the building.

Pearce Signs factory, Broadstairs, Kent.

On the north western edge of the Broadstairs boundary is Westwood and for more than 40 years until 2005 stood the Pearce Signs offices and factory at the junction with Margate and Ramsgate Roads. The main picture was taken in 1983 while the inset shows a rear view of demolition in 2005.

Pearce Signs had a 200 year long history and was once Europe's largest sign maker. The family owned company moved to Margate in 2004 but closed down the following year – with the loss of more than 100 jobs. The Westwood site has since given way to a DIY 'shed' and other retail outlets.

Asda's Broadstairs store in Westwood Road stands on the site formerly occupied by the North Foreland Radio station. Not a music channel, but run by the Post Office and latterly BT to provide vital ship to shore radio links for merchant vessels. Here John McFarlane is at the main console during 1966.

Given the anonymous address of 96 Rumfields Road, North Foreland Radio was one of a chain of 11 stations. It moved from a site by the lighthouse in 1929 and operated until closure in 1991. Using the call sign GNF, it was making more than 55,000 calls to ships during the 1960s. Here, S Abram checks a loudspeaker terminal.

In 1963, five girls in the sixth form at Dane Court School were carnival queens or princesses in different parts of Thanet. In the main picture we see them in uniform at the school gate while, inset, they are in their tiaras and posh frocks. From left are Susan Moroney, Patricia Clark, Veronica Higgins, Edwina Black and Joyce Eteen.

During the Napoleonic Wars the tower of St Peter's church was a naval lookout and is still allowed to fly the White Ensign. Just inside the gate is an 18th century memorial to Richard Joy, who until earlier in 2007, was thought to be the Kentish Samson. It his brother William who has this title and he was buried at sea in 1734.

The Ford Prefect car plants this photograph at the junction of St Peter's High Street with Church Street in the 1950s. The village's medicinal needs were met by DT Evans, the chemist on the corner, while opposite, medicines of a different kind were on tap in the Red Lion, then a Tomson & Wotton house.

The High Street was closed for a time in early 2007 but the chemist was still in business, having extended into a former newsagent, as was the pub. Further along the High Street used to be Creasy's slaughterhouse and adjoining grocery which was the only place in the village allowed to sell wines and spirits in the 1920s.

The 11th century flint built parish church dominates in this 1909 view of St Peter's High Street. The pub on the left was the Crown & Thistle and dated from the 17th century. It was demolished in the 1950s to be replaced by two shops. The entrance to Jennings' butcher's can be seen on the right.

The history of St Peter's is expertly recreated by costumed volunteers presenting the weekly village tour during the summer months. The tours began in 1995 and since then more than 15,000 have enjoyed the 90 minute walk. The peeler stands by the St Peter's sign which dates from the 1920s. Its design won the £1,000 first prize in a competion run by the Daily Mail for the country's best village sign.

Arguably Broadstairs' most famous son was Sir Edward Heath, Prime Minister between 1970 and 1974. He was born of humble parentage in the ground floor flat, seen left, at 1 Holmwood Villas in Albion Road, St Peter's, on 9 July 1916. Once old enough he attended the village school (pictured above in 1970). In 1926 the Heath family moved to King Edward Avenue in Broadstairs and Sir Edward soon went on to Chatham House School in Ramsgate. A model pupil, he won a scholarship at Balliol College, Oxford, in 1935 to read politics, philosophy and economics.

Sir Edward became Conservative MP for Bexley & Sidcup in February 1950, the seat he held throughout his 51 year long Parliamentary career. Despite the pressures of various ministerial roles and party leadership, Sir Edward spent as much time as he could in Broadstairs to visit his parents and indulge his passions for sailing and music. He is seen, below, in a small craft off Broadstairs in the 1960s with friend Rex Walden. Later, Sir Edward sailed his ocean going yacht Morning Cloud II to victory in the tough 1969 Sydney-Hobart race off Australia. He also captained Britain's Admiral's Cup team in 1971.

In 1936 Sir Edward established Broadstairs' annual pre-Christmas carol party. He is seen, above, conducting during one of these occasions at the Grand Ballroom. As PM he is best remembered for taking Britain into the Common Market, now the European Union. He fell from grace after losing two elections following the miner's strike and three day week of 1973 to be replaced as party leader by Baroness Margaret Thatcher. Sir Edward died at his home in Salisbury on 17 July 2005, aged 89. By then he was a multi-millionaire.

The New Wash House wasn't a public bath but one of several hand laundries in the vicinity. Shirts and collars were a speciality. A rising platform appears to have been added to the extreme left hand window. The view dates from the early 20th century. By the 1930s Albion House had been converted into flats.

Bereft of cars, Vicarage Street was a peaceful place when this view was taken in the 1930s. On the right, halfway up is the entrance to Oaklands Court. Vicarage Street was known as St Peter's Street in the 1861 census but had swopped to its former name when the next one was taken 10 years after.

Along Convent Road heading towards Kingsgate, was Glyn House School, seen here in the 1930s. Originally built in 1913 as Brondesbury Ladies' School for 'daughters of professional men', exams were optional. In the 1950s the principal was Sir Wilfred Garrett. The YMCA took over the place afterwards.

By the 1960s, the site had been renamed Kingsgate College, the rear view shown inset, and was largely used for teaching English to overseas students. Since 1990, it has been the home of teenaged Japanese students from the Shumei Foundation who come to this country for short English courses.

Port Regis, taking the Latin name for Kingsgate, was built in 1764 by eccentric landowner Lord Holland. Originally named the Convent of St Mildred, and hence its address in Convent Road, it was actually home to his retired estate workers. Later, it was a charitable institution offering shelter for poor women of the parish.

Port Regis became a boys' school in 1921 when bought by Sir Milsom Rees, King George V's laryngologist and in the years before World War Two William Joyce – later the infamous Lord Haw Haw – taught English here. From 1945 until the late 1970s Port Regis was run as a convent for 'delicate girls' by the Belgian order of the Daughters of the Cross. Today, Port Regis is a retirement home as well as a Montessouri nursery school.

The Noble Captain Digby was built between 1763 and 1768 as one of Lord Holland's follies. It was originally half of the Bede House, which fell into the sea in 1809. Steps nearby led to the beach and were used by smugglers. By 1909 tea parties were being catered for 'in any number at short notice' (see inset).

The pub was named after Lord Holland's favourite nephew who built a navy career catching smugglers! Shrimp brand beers were for sale in the 1930s (see inset) and were advertised prominently. The Captain Digby was bought in 1979 by Frank Thorley as one of his first pubs and is still part of Thorley Taverns.

Judging by the lack of sea defences on the cliff below Kingsgate Castle, this is an early view of the area. The castle has a rustic quality about it – which its builder Lord Holland intended. He lived at Holland House, the white building on the right, from 1760 and wanted to awaken to a view of a castle – one of nine follies he had built.

Owing to tree growth, one has to walk further along the headland to get an uncluttered view of Kingsgate Bay these days. The round tower is the only original part of the castle remaining. The castle has grown while the cliffs have been shored up further to prevent everything going seawards.

Clifftop walkers setting out from Kingsgate to Fayreness soon meet another Holland folly. An ancient tower, thought to date from the 16th century and falsely rumoured to have been the grave of King Vortigern – who invited the Saxons to land in Kent – is surrounded by the flint built Arx Rouchim.

Modelled on King Henry VIII's castle at Deal, the Arx Rouchim is also known as the Temple of Neptune or Neptune's Tower. The old tower has long since collapsed leaving the Arx standing alone. A coastguard hut also stood here as recently as the 1920s. Now, the Arx provides a convenient windbreak for golfers.

This is Fitzroy Avenue, Kingsgate, probably in the late 1920s or early 1930s and was one of a profusion of pleasant avenues that sprang up in the area during the first three decades of the 20th century as people continued to move to the coast for bracing sea air and sunshine.

Now, inevitably, Fitzroy Avenue is more heavily developed. Well tended hedges have given way to high walls and iron gates on the left while bungalows gobbled up the open land on the right. There is a still an unhurried atmosphere while some properties in this road command seven figure sale prices.

Kingsgate Avenue was originally built to appeal to the professional and upper middle classes and is seen here around 1930. Dogs and walkers were safe to roam in the middle of the traffic free road. The properties in the centre distance are in Percy Avenue.

Although taken in early 2007, this picture is already out of date as the balconied property on the extreme left has since been demolished to make way for a block of eight apartments! It is just one of a number of properties to be redeveloped in Kingsgate Avenue as the price of land escalates.

A sole Austin trundles along Percy Avenue, pictured just prior to the Second World War. The road was named after Percy Snowden who developed parts of this area and these detached houses were built for the middle classes. However, 131, Rose Lawn, stands out with its own blue plaque to someone famous.

Rose Lawn was home for 30 years to Frank Richards, the pen name of Charles Hamilton, who created owlish schoolboy Billy Bunter and friends of Greyfriars School. The author is pictured wearing trademark skull cap and lighting his pipe. When he died in late1961, his housekeeper, Edith Hood, phoned local journalist Bill Evans asking 'Do you think anyone would be interested?' The story soon made international headlines!

Arguably Lord Holland's most spectacular folly, Kingsgate Castle was originally stables and grooms' accommodation to his Holland House when first built in 1766. Extensive alterations were made in the 1860s and 1903. Lord Avebury, who introduced the Bank Holiday, was a subsequent owner.

Although the castle is divided into 32 privately owned flats today, Reuben Peace purchased the place from Lady Avebury in 1922, after her husband's death, to run it as a smart hotel. Its summertime fancy dress balls were very popular in this era. The castle was turned into flats during the 1950s.

Pictured soon after its opening in 1957, the Castle Keep Hotel was built on a neighbouring plot to Kingsgate Castle but was a separate entity. The best of its 20 bedrooms were available on weekly terms for 22 guineas (£23.10) at the time. Bed and breakfast was at least one guinea (£1.05).

The hotel was extended during the 1970s to offer 40 bedrooms and a large open air swimming pool. Owners at the time were Peter and Pat Stoneham who successfully built up the business into what became Thanet's only three star hotel. Swish cabaret evenings were a popular feature by the middle of the decade.

Come on in, the water's lovely could be the caption to this 1975 press picture of two lovelies enjoying Castle Keep's new pool. There was little doubt this was one of the best places for a dip in the area. Many showbiz stars stayed at the hotel when appearing in local theatres including Morecambe & Wise.

There's no sign of the hotel and its pool these days. Castle Keep closed down in the late 1990s and lay derelict for some time. Since then, the Bayside Heights apartments have been built in their place. Work was still continuing on this block in spring 2007, close to where the pool used to be.

Contrary to popular belief, Joss Bay does not get its name from smuggler Joss Snelling, but is more likely to be the other way around. The bay, seen here as a popular sun trap in the 1930s, was used by the tenants of what was Joss Farm for collecting seaweed in the 17th century, before Snelling was born.

Coastal erosion has made its presence felt in the intervening 70 years between this and facing image with the sand blowing higher up the unprotected part of the cliffs. It was at Joss Bay that the very first attempts at developing radar, known as listening ears or sound mirrors, were made during the First World War.

One of Broadstairs most notable residents and benefactors was media baron Lord Northcliffe, the founder of the Daily Mail in 1896 and later owner of The Times. He lived at Elmwood, seen here in the late 1950s, in Reading Street village, from 1891 until his death as a Viscount in 1922, aged only 57.

During the First World War, Northcliffe was Minister for Propaganda. In February 1917, German destroyers tried to bombard his house but in doing so struck Rose Cottage, left, killing a mother and two daughters. The house has been known as Remembrance Cottage ever since, the round window filling the hole made by the shell. Close by today is the former village school – note the weather vane!

The Hearts of Oak Benefit Society built a brand new home for its members in1938 on the site of Callis Court, the one time mansion of Harry H Marks MP in Callis Court Road. The home cost £50,000 to build and equip and provided for 50 convalescents in relaxing surroundings incorporating some of Callis Court's gardens.

The 1930s building made way for another purpose built home, this time for the Royal British Legion, in 1990. Residents transferred from Maurice House in Westgate, bringing the name with them. The two lower pictures give an idea of 1950s accommodation when under the stewardship of Hearts of Oak.

There has been a beacon of light shone from the North Foreland since 1499, making it the oldest light still in use in England. A tower of chalk blocks with a brazier on top was in use when the Spanish Armada sailed past in 1588. The present light was built in 1691 but has been considerably altered since.

The lighthouse, pictured in the 1920s soon after it was electrified, is around 90 feet tall. It was the last in the UK to be permanently manned until 1998 when it was converted to automatic operation at a ceremony attended by the Duke of Edinburgh. The lighthouse's main beam is visible for 19 sea miles.

Virtually opposite the lighthouse was the Dutch Tea House. Originally the North Foreland Tea House, it was a pleasant place for a cuppa after a bracing walk from the centre of Broadstairs. Waitresses in Dutch costume attended customers. Open all year round, it was doubling as a sub Post Office in 1956.

The Dutch Tea House also took in paying guests and by the mid 1950s offered terms from eight guineas (£8.40) per week, quite pricey when other guest houses were often charging £1 per person less. These days the building has reverted to a private house, secluded by tall hedges and trees.

Broadstairs has been home to numerous private schools including St Stephen's College, one of few catering solely for girls. It was established in 1867 and moved to its premises in North Foreland Road at the end of the 1960s. In 1970 gifts of Arabian horses were made to the school by Major General Nasser, brother-in-law of King Hussein of Jordan. Below, headmistress Miss Joan Selby-Lowndes has unloaded one of the newly arrived animals from its box in front of an admiring crowd.

Above, the Major General's daughters, Zein, Nour and Rajha, were pupils at the school and were quick to welcome the horses to their quarters. The animals went a long way to establishing a successful riding school for the 125 college pupils. Primary age girls were boarded at a house named Wynstow, across the road from St Stephen's, and used a tunnel to get to and from the main buildings each day.

Here we see the younger pupils of Form Two during an English lesson in1970. By the time St Stephen's closed in 1991, girls from all over the world had passed through its gates. The site was derelict for some years but has made way for the houses of Foreland Heights. The most recent development has been the creation of the attractive Broadhall Manor apartments block on ground formerly occupied by the stables.

Just to one side of the North Foreland estate lay Thanet Place, the home of meat millionaire Sir Edmund Vestey who, with his brother, owned the Blue Star Shipping Line and the Union Cold Storage Co. The Italianate style palace was completed in 1929 for £100,000. This view was captured in 1958, five years after Sir Edmund's death, just as St Mary's children's home was established here. Now, a residential home for older people, its seven acre grounds, inset, have been built on to create Thanet Place Gardens.

The Metropolitan Convalescent Home in Lanthorne Road, seen here in the 1930s, cared for children with TB and similar conditions. It was demolished in 1986 to make way for Lanthorne Court, caring for profoundly disabled young people. At the top we can see the playing fields of the former Stone House School and on the left is the building which became the Kingfisher Children's Centre in 1997.

In 1936 Miss Enid Briggs, her sister Phyllis and their mother bought five acres of land in Seaview Road to create a retirement home for horses and donkeys which they named The Ranch. Once a horse was past its prime and no longer able to work, it was able to live out its days at this equine haven.

Beach donkeys and milk float horses were among the residents of The Ranch and lapped up the care and attention Miss Briggs and her supporters provided. Miss Briggs, pictured feeding Tony the donkey, was also an accomplished local film maker in the 1930s. The Ranch continued until Miss Briggs died in 1973.

Many of the buildings fronting the East Cliff – which overlooks Stone Bay – date from when the Esplanade was built in 1894. Judging by this early 20th century view, the beach was an ideal place for hunting crabs in the many rock pools formed here.

Redevelopment in the 1960s and the effects of cliff erosion have changed the landscape of the East Cliff. The beach is far sandier today while access to it has been made easier with a twisting slope down. Inset, the promenade was built in 1970 at a cost of £350,000, much of it paid from grants.

Quite why an invalid shelter should be the focus of attention for a 1950s post card is not easy to fathom but we have a good view along Rectory Road, looking towards the sea on a quiet day. The road gets its name from the fact the rectory to Holy Trinity Church was built here in 1871.

Rectory Road is still a tree lined avenue and there is still a shelter to focus our eye on at the far end in this contemporary view. On the right hand side, before reaching the shelter is Copperfield Court, a modern block of flats which was built on the site of the prestigious Esplanade Hotel.

The Vale, formerly The Lynch, and off Ramsgate Road, was home of the Collegiate School in the 1860s, a high class establishment for young ladies and gentlemen. The spire of the congregational church can be clearly seen in this 1950s view which also shows a number of guest houses along the same side of the road.

Guest houses still abound here, the Oakfield retains its name from the 1950s, while the church has become the United Reformed. The Vale took on its name when houses forming Inverness Terrace, further along on the left, were built for the servants of Princess, later Queen, Victoria when she stayed at Pierremont Hall.

The Yarrow Home for Convalescent Children, Broadstairs.

The Yarrow Home is now Thanet College's original building and has been grade two listed since 1998. It was established by shipbuilder and philanthropist Sir Alfred Yarrow in 1894 for £35,000 to care for up to 50 youngsters of the 'better classes' recovering from illness. The weekly fee then was five shillings (25p).

TAIT CONVALESCENT HOME

Tait Convalescent Home was built in 1875 and shared six acres of ground with St Peter's Orphanage in Lanthorne Road. This dated from 1869, when named after the wife of Dr Tait, Archbishop of Canterbury. They had just lost five daughters in six weeks to scarlet fever. Both buildings were demolished in 1953.

Carnivals have long been an essential part of summer in Broadstairs and are led by the queen and her princesses. Miss Broadstairs was a coveted title and among previous winners, from left, are 1960's holder Yvonne Mackenzie, 1961, Denise Collins and 1962, Lesley Pentress with the Morelli Trophy.

Miss Broadstairs in 1965 was 21 year old Mary Smith, a young cousin of future Prime Minister Sir Edward Heath. Mary is seen boarding her float ahead of that year's procession. The vehicle has been parked in Fordoun Road at the rear of JC Morrison's Broadway garage where it was normally stored. Stacey's Fish Bar in the background, in St Peter's Park Road, was the first chip shop in the town.

In this view from a mid 1960s procession, possibly in Granville Road, Morelli's was represented by a large ice cream cone. In fact it was a glass fibre body mounted on the chassis of a Mini car. Note the council's Visit Broadstairs Dormobile in front. In the off season it would travel northern England promoting the town.

Getting in on the Broadstairs carnival scene in 1971 was the Coal Merchant Federation, who with its own beauty queen, was anxious to ensure people installed only coal fired central heating in their homes. Margate merchant KG Attwell provided the lorry. Sadly, the coal merchant queen is unknown.

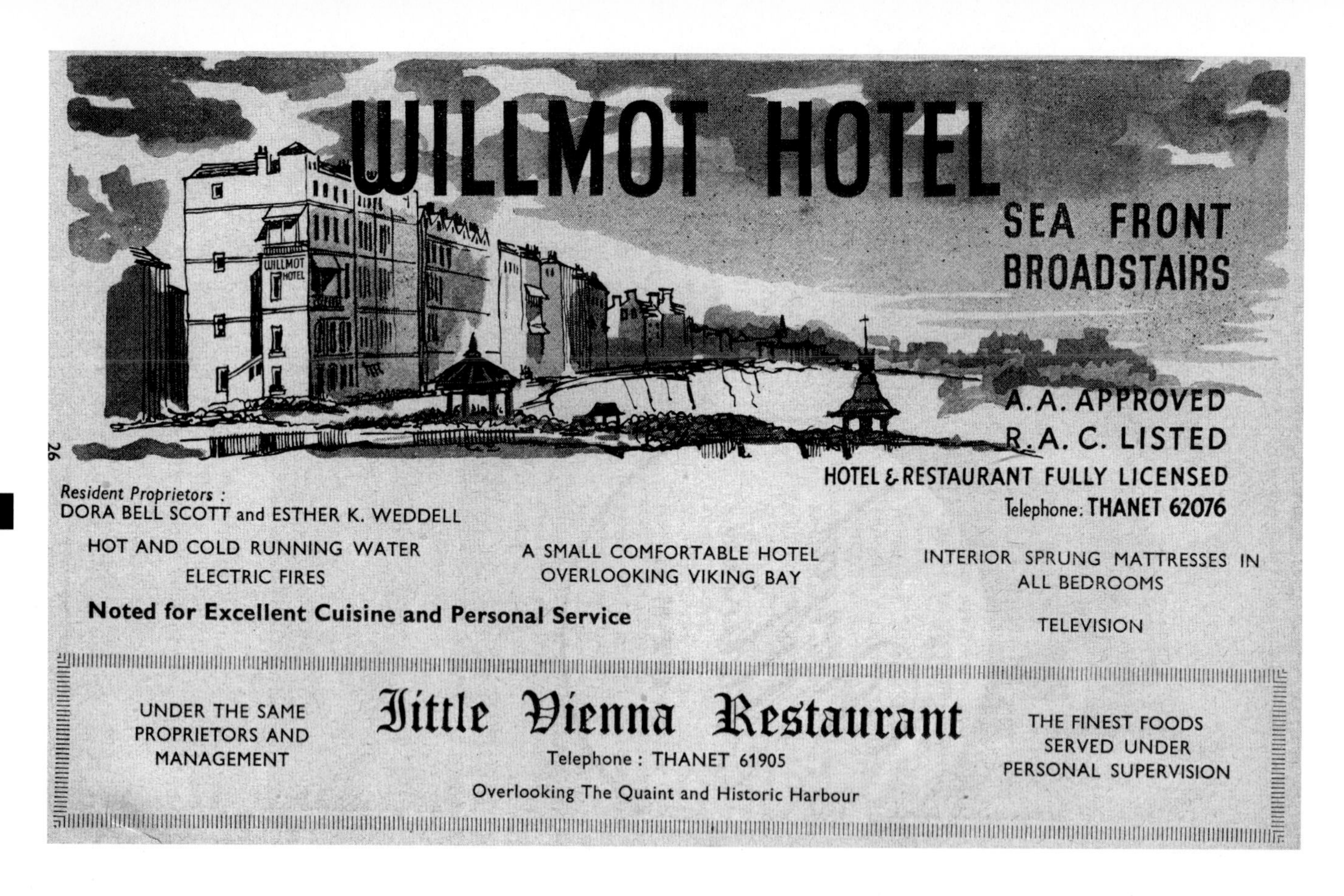

From the 1956 Broadstairs holiday guide. Little Vienna later became the Mad Chef's Bistro in the 1980s by the jetty and is now a private house.

Telephone:
Broadstairs
1166
(2 Lines)

Telegrams:
Castlemere,
Broadstairs

CASTLEMERE is situated on the Western Esplanade of Broadstairs. It has a Southern aspect, open sea views and extensive gardens. The Hotel offers singular advantages to those seeking sunshine, tonic air, rest and competent attention, and is open all the year round.

Castlemere is centrally heated throughout, the bedrooms equipped with hot and cold running water and gas or electric fires.

Personal Proprietors - Mrs. KNIGHT-BRUCE, Miss ELIZABETH BENNETT

CASTLEMERE
BROADSTAIRS

ISLE OF THANET

The Castlemere Hotel, like many other larger establishments, was a regular advertiser in the annual holiday guide. This one originates from 1946 when four digit phone numbers were still in use.

Fayreness Hotel

Kingsgate — Nr. BROADSTAIRS

A PERSONAL WELCOME AWAITS YOU AT THIS CHARMING AND DISTINCTIVE HOTEL SITUATED ON THE CLIFFS OVERLOOKING A DELIGHTFUL SANDY BAY AND HAVING BEAUTIFUL SEA VIEWS

●

INDIVIDUAL TASTES AND FAMILIES CATERED FOR SPECIAL TERMS FOR CHILDREN

●

Excellent Cuisine Spacious Lawns
Hot and Cold Running Water in all Bedrooms, some with Private Bathrooms

●

FULLY LICENSED

Terms from £10 . 10 . 0 per week

Please write for illustrated Brochure to the Resident Proprietors
W/Cmdr. and Mrs. J. ROTHWELL

Telephone : Thanet 61001

The Fayreness Hotel at Kingsgate is now part of the Thorley Taverns chain but was independently owned in 1956 when this advert was first published.

THE

GRAND BALLROOM AND SWIMMING POOL

(Recently acquired by Mr. Tom Glennan of Dundee)

This Beautiful Ballroom has been completely redecorated, refurnished and equipped for

DINNER-DANCES
WEDDING RECEPTIONS
PUBLIC DANCING, ETC.

MODERN AND OLD TIME DANCERS will be catered for throughout the year. Dance Organisers should ask for Terms

THE SWIMMING POOL will be open during the Summer Season

Refreshments Available

From the same year, the Grand Ballroom, a major social centre in the town, was doing its bit to attract visitors to the area. The adjoining Grand Hotel had by now been converted into flats.

"Bishops Bourne"

HIGH-CLASS PRIVATE HOTEL

Telephone : Thanet 61938

Kingsgate Avenue, Kingsgate-on-Sea, near Broadstairs

Two minutes Botany Bay. Easy reach of Kingsgate Bay, Joss Bay, and North Foreland Golf Course. Two acres Garden. Hard Tennis Court. Putting Green. Private Car Accommodation

Interior Spring Mattresses. H. and C. all rooms. Separate Tables. Superb Lounge. Excellent Cuisine. Own Poultry, etc.

WINTER TERMS : From 6½ gns. per week according to month

Your Every Comfort Assured

Under Personal Supervision of the Resident Proprietors Mr. and Mrs. CYRIL HOOK

AUTHORITATIVELY RECOMMENDED

Comfort and relaxation seemed a certainty for holidaymakers staying at Bishops Bourne in Kingsgate Avenue during the 1950s.

"From motives of philanthropy"

CHARLES DICKENS wrote of the Shopkeepers of Broadstairs "They all do business, it is to be presumed, from motives of philanthropy...........their interest in strangers, and their politeness, bespeak their amiable nature."

100 years later, at LANES, we try to justify these remarks of Charles Dickens.

At LANES, you will find Books, Stationery, Leather Goods, View Postcards, Maps and many goods suitable for gifts or personal use. Visitors are welcomed at our Circulating Library.

Stationers : Booksellers : Printers

45 HIGH STREET, BROADSTAIRS *Tel.*: 61313 (2 lines)

P.S. See our exclusive range of Ivorex Plaques of Dickens and other subjects.

THE LOCAL ESTATE AGENTS

We have the Key of YOUR Home by the Sea

If you are contemplating a Residence by the Sea either for a month, a season, or permanently, we will be pleased to send detailed particulars of all available residences to be let or sold, furnished or unfurnished

B. J. PEARSON & SON

F.A.L.P.A.

AUCTIONEERS, SURVEYORS, LAND and ESTATE AGENTS

STATION GATES :: :: BROADSTAIRS

- *Phone :* Thanet 61283
- *Grams :* "Pearson, Broadstairs"

Branches at : CLIFTONVILLE, MARGATE, RAMSGATE, BIRCHINGTON-ON-SEA, KINGSGATE-ON-SEA, MINSTER, THANET, AND LONDON

Both Lanes printers and BJ Pearson are still in business. The estate agent still trades from its office close to the railway station while Lanes concentrates on commercial printing at Pysons Road estate.

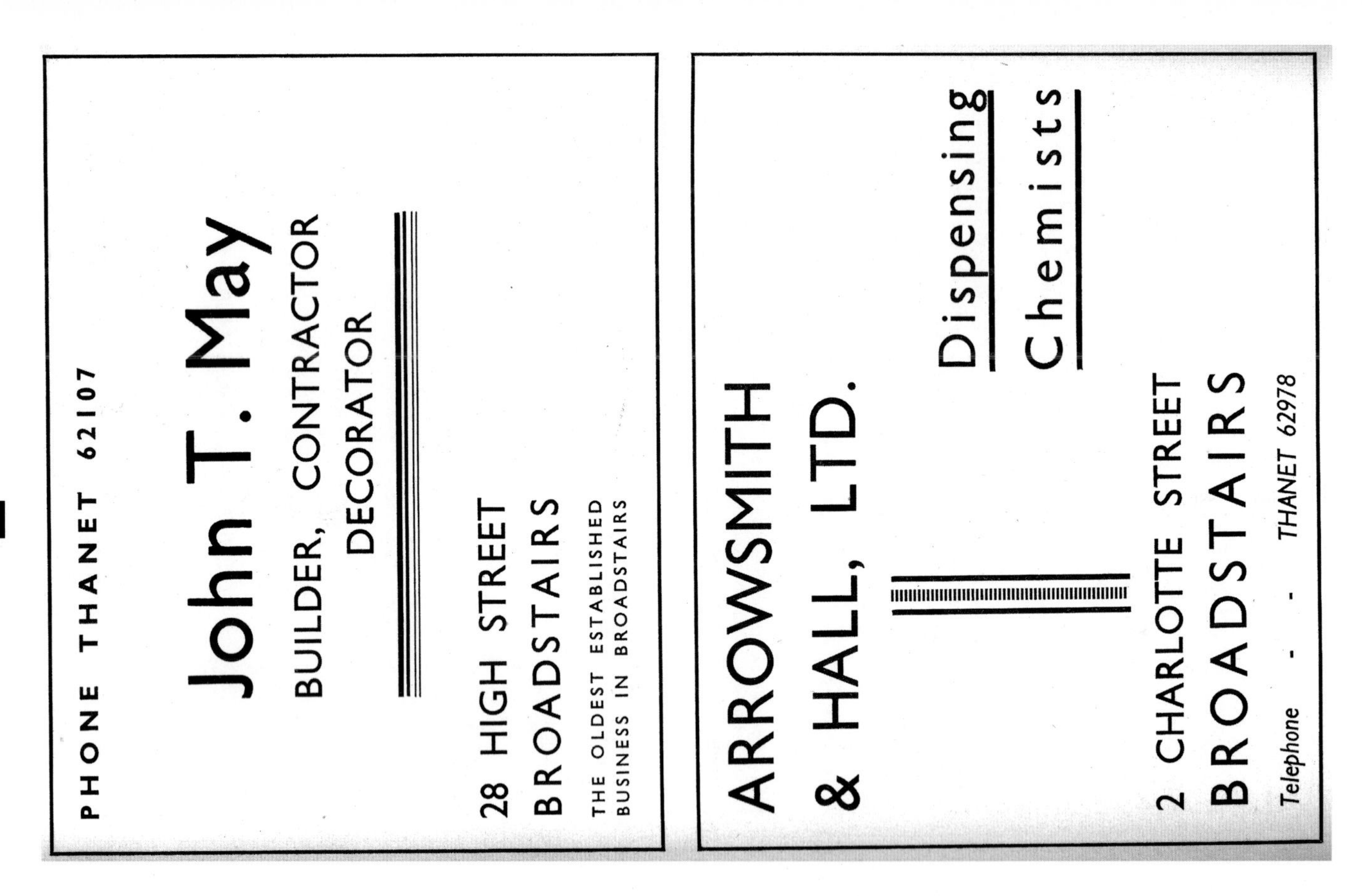

It wasn't just guest houses and hotels who advertised in the holiday guides. Other local business joined in as well, partly out of civic duty perhaps but also to win visitors' business.

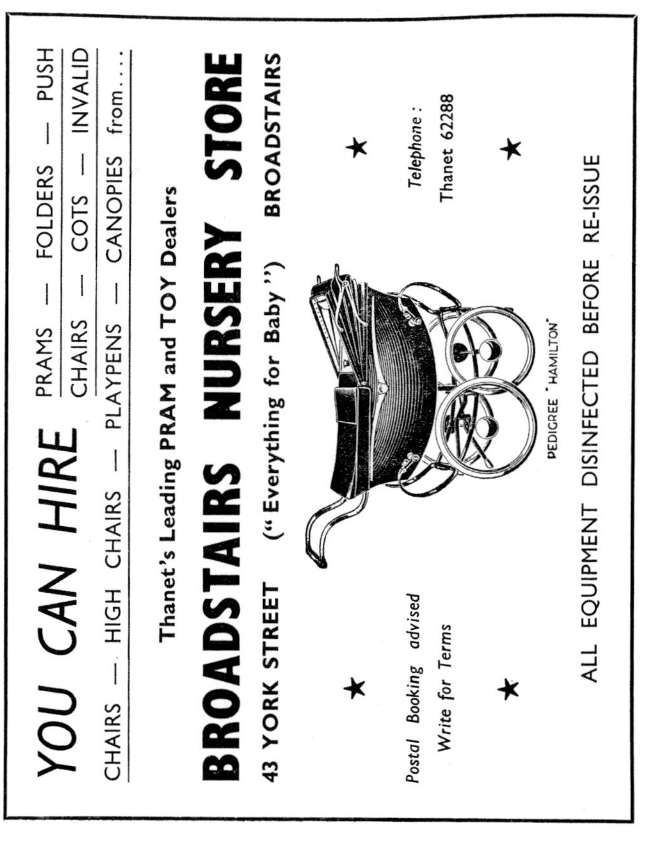

During Coronation Year 1953, grocers' Vyes promoted its teas while a nursery store in Albion Street was keen to boost its equipment hire business – emphasising disinfection between uses!

Photographic credits and bibliography

The author is indebted to the following for their help in the production of this book:
Mrs Marian Evans for the loan of her postcard collection used extensively here
The Morelli family for the loan of photographs on pages 38, 40, 41 and 150
Margate Museum for lending photograph with Annette Mills on page 47
Broadstairs Folk Week for loaning photographs on pages 44 and 45 taken
by the Isle of Thanet Gazette

Contemporary photographs by Nick Evans

Bibliography:

Kelly's Isle of Thanet Directories 1934, 1938 and 1951
AA Hotel Handbook 1938
Broadstairs official guides 1946, 1953 and 1956
AA Members' Handbook 1957
RAC Guide & Handbook 1958
The Story of Broadstairs & St Peter's by James Bird 1974
Old Broadstairs by Michael David Mirams 1986
Broadstairs & St Peter's In Old Photographs by John Whyman 1990
Early Broadstairs & St Peter's by Barrie Wootton 1992
Various articles from Isle of Thanet Gazette and East Kent Times

We've taken all reasonable steps to ensure the correct people are credited for the use of their photographs but any issues arising can be addressed to the author at Bygone Publishing, PO Box 201, Whitstable, Kent CT5 1WT and he will be happy to consider corrections for any future editions.